Phil Young was born in Liverpool. A graduate of Leeds University Workshop Theatre, he was the inaugural winner of the R.S.C. Buzz Goodbody Award for his production of Georg Kaiser's *Gas* at the 1976 National Student Drama Festival. He co-founded the Mutable Theatre and is a former associate director of the Liverpool Everyman and the Leeds Playhouse. His London work includes: Pirandello's *Six Characters in Search of an Author* (Greenwich, 1979); Tom Robertson's *A Row in the House* (Orange Tree, 1979); Athol Fugard's *The Island* (Croydon Warehouse, 1980); and Dennis Kennedy's *Telephone Man* (Almost Free Theatre, 1980). In 1981 he founded his own company, Public Property, and presented *Creatures of Another Kind* by David Halliwell, *In Kanada* by David Clough and *Crystal Clear* at the Old Red Lion pub theatre in Islington. In 1982 he directed a national tour of Mike Leigh's *Goose-Pimples*, with whom he had previously worked as an assistant director on an experimental project at the R.S.C. He is married to the actress Deborah Black.

Anthony Allen trained at the London Academy of Music and Dramatic Art and went on to do a wide variety of work in theatre, films and television. He was a co-founder of the Shared Experience Theatre Company. His leading roles in television include parts in *A Crack of Heaven* for 'Love Story', *The Square of Three* for 'Armchair Theatre', *The Launderette*, *A Collier's Friday Night*, *Father Brown*, *General Hospital*, *Marked Personal*, *Crown Court* and *Rooms*. His film roles include parts in *No Hard Feelings*, *Flame*, *The Rape* and *Glass Shot*. He is a member of the Actors' Institute, New York, and the Actors' Centre, London.

Diana Barrett trained at the London Academy of Music and Dramatic Art after taking a sociology degree at London University. She became a member of the community theatre companies' Common Stock and Bubble Theatre, touring mainly in the London area. Most of her career has been spent with groups that work collaboratively on devised or new plays. In 1975 Mike Alfreds asked her to be a founder of Shared Experience and she appeared in *An Arabian Night*, which is when she first worked with Anthony Allen. She spent four years with Greenwich Young People's Theatre devising and performing in theatre-in-education programmes. She recently appeared with Monstrous Regiment in *Yoga Class*.

Philomena McDonagh has worked in repertory companies all over the country, playing diverse parts including Amanda in *Private Lives*, Alison in *Look Back in Anger*, Fay in *Loot* and Virginia in *Saturday, Sunday, Monday*. She played a leading role in *Lost Worlds* at the National Theatre in 1978, Portia in *The Merchant of Venice* at St George's Theatre and a leading role in the much acclaimed production of *In Kanada* at the Old Red Lion. Her television work includes *World's End*, *Bloomfield*, *Happy*, Trevor Griffiths's play *Through the Night*, a spell in the B.B.C. series *Angels*, and she was a regular character in another B.B.C. series, *Grange Hill*. Her film work includes *The Errand* and *Ascendancy*.

DEVISED BY
PHIL YOUNG

CRYSTAL CLEAR

Crystal Clear was originally created through
improvisation with Anthony Allen,
Diana Barrett and Philomena McDonagh

PENGUIN BOOKS

Penguin Books Ltd, Harmondsworth, Middlesex, England
Penguin Books, 625 Madison Avenue, New York, New York 10022, U.S.A.
Penguin Books Australia Ltd, Ringwood, Victoria, Australia
Penguin Books Canada Ltd, 2801 John Street, Markham, Ontario, Canada L3R 1B4
Penguin Books (N.Z.) Ltd, 182–190 Wairau Road, Auckland 10, New Zealand

First published 1983

Professional performing rights of this play are controlled by
A. D. Peters & Co. Ltd of 10 Buckingham Street, London, WC2N 6BU.
Rights of performance by amateurs are controlled by Samuel French Limited,
26 Southampton Street, London, WC2E 7JE. The publication of this play in
French's Acting Edition must not be taken to imply that it is available for
performance.

Made and printed in Great Britain by
Richard Clay (The Chaucer Press) Ltd, Bungay, Suffolk
Set in Monophoto Bembo

TO DEBORAH

PREFACE

The idea for *Crystal Clear* came whilst staying at a meditation centre in Wiltshire in May 1982. I shared a room with Dennis, who had been blind for a number of years due to diabetes. From 4.30 a.m. to 9.30 p.m. with three breaks for meals I sat in the meditation hall with my eyes closed trying to meditate. I wasn't very good at it. You are supposed to empty your mind of all thought. I quickly began to fill mine with ideas for a play.

Weeks later I spent some time with Dennis at his home in Weston-super-Mare. He gave me my first opportunity to rid myself of the ignorant notions I had about the life experiences of people who cannot see.

I returned to London faced with the marvellous problem of producing the conditions whereby a play could be created from nothing. There was no script and no writer. I had to find actors who would be attracted not by the money (because there wasn't any, save basic expenses) but by the nature of the work. Fortunately I had worked with Philomena and Diana recently and about two months before we started I met Tony at a workshop organized by The Actors' Institute.

I found a large, peaceful rehearsal space above a pub for £40 a week (very cheap!), and to equip it we emptied our homes of furniture, crockery, cutlery and bedding etc., whilst Guy investigated the many skips and jumble sales of north London. In the end we were able to 'build' the homes of Jane, Thomasina and Richard within which most of our improvisations over the next four months would take place. Once Tony and Philomena had had their special lenses fitted, which would block out their sight, we were on the way.

In developing this play we have had meetings with many people. We have all been inspired by their willingness to reveal their most private thoughts and feelings. *Crystal Clear* has been created by them as well as us.

Phil Young

Crystal Clear was first performed at the Old Red Lion, Islington, London, on 23 November 1982 with the following cast:

RICHARD   ANTHONY ALLEN
THOMASINA   PHILOMENA MCDONAGH
JANE   DIANA BARRETT

DIRECTOR   PHIL YOUNG
ASSISTANT DIRECTOR   GUY FAWKES
STAGE MANAGER   CLARE SCHRADER

The first performance at Wyndham's Theatre, London, was on 23 February 1983.

Crystal Clear was inspired by
Dennis Carling and is dedicated to him.

CHARACTERS

RICHARD

THOMASINA

JANE

The play is set in London in the present day.
All five scenes take place in Richard's flat.
The play runs without an interval.

SCENE 1
RICHARD'S FLAT

Situated on the first floor above an old antique/junk shop which is rarely, if ever, open, on the edge of the 'City' area of London.

It consists of one room, a small kitchen, and across the corridor from the entrance to the flat a bathroom/toilet.

The flat contains, to the left as you look at the stage, a large Georgian bookcase; along the top wall, moving right, the kitchen entrance, a table and shelves, a chest of drawers, a futon (a low Japanese bed), a home-made rack for clothes. Along the right-hand wall, a small waste-paper bin, a music stand and stereo system perched on two tea-chests.

Towards the left of the bottom of the futon, near the bookcase, an Edwardian easy-chair, and next to this a cardboard box which RICHARD *uses as a side-table.*

The walls abound with pictures, mainly water-colours, and the flat has a half-decorated air about it with lots of boxes around both sides of the room, still unpacked.

RICHARD *is heard guiding* THOMASINA *through the rubbish stacked in the hall outside the flat.*

RICHARD *and* THOMASINA *enter. The room is dark.*

RICHARD: Right, come in. Now, if you'll just wait there, I'll turn on the light.

   [*Switches on light, and closes door.*]

Da-daa! So, this is what's been keeping me busy for the past few weeks. What are your first impressions?

THOMASINA: It feels very spacious.

RICHARD: Spacious? Yes, well, it is quite. Probably what attracted me to it in the first place. Anything else?

THOMASINA [*sniffing the air*]: Well, it smells a bit musty.

RICHARD: Oh dear, does it? Well, it hasn't been lived in for some time. You see, so it needs . . .

THOMASINA: But it feels nice. It has a nice feel.

RICHARD: Oh good. Well, I'm glad you like it. Can I take your coat, Tom?

THOMASINA: Yes, yes.

   [*He helps her remove her coat and hangs it up on the door.*]

RICHARD: Now, madam, we have a variety of seating arrangements for you to choose from. We have a swivel chair, an armchair, and we even have a futon!

THOMASINA: A futon! How trendy!

RICHARD: Yes, it is rather, isn't it. Trouble is all the trendiness disappears as soon as you cover it with bedclothes.

THOMASINA: Where is it?

RICHARD: Just here, I'll show you. Mind your shins, it's very low.

[*He takes her hand and leads her across to the bed.*]

THOMASINA: Oh, I see. [*Investigates it with her hands*] It's got a sort of frame underneath; is that to let the air in?

RICHARD: Yes, it stops all the condensation and, er, mushrooms building up.

THOMASINA [*she laughs and then stands up*]: Do you know, I always thought a futon was a sort of duvet.

RICHARD: No, no, it's just a mattress, except it's more like sleeping on a slab of bread pudding. Here, feel how solid that is.

[*She bends down and feels it.*]

THOMASINA: Oh yes. What else is in this room, Richard?

RICHARD: What else is in this room, Richard! Ah, yes, over here is my brand-new trendy stereo system.

[*He moves to it.*]

Er, over here.

[*He takes her hand.*]

You don't mind me pulling you around?

THOMASINA: Not at all. [*Feeling first the deck*] Oh yes. [*Then feeling tea-chest*] It's on a tea-chest.

[*Pause.*]

RICHARD: Yes, I've got a couple of, er, trendy tea-chests there.

THOMASINA [*feeling what she touches*]: Headphones. [*Touching amplifier*]. Amplifier.

RICHARD: Er, yes, the . . . stack.

THOMASINA [*feeling her way along*]: Oh, you've got a music stand! What do you play?

RICHARD: I'm just trying to get some John Lennon down at the moment.

THOMASINA: What instrument?

RICHARD: Guitar.

THOMASINA: Oh, I'm learning to play the mouth-organ.

RICHARD: Really! Well, maybe we should 'Come Together'.

THOMASINA [*stretching her hands forwards*]: What's here?

RICHARD: A temporary clothes-rack.

THOMASINA: Oh, yes [*touches her way along it*].

[*She touches a plant on it.*]

RICHARD: That's a plant.

THOMASINA: I know it's a plant.

[*They laugh.*]

[*She reaches up the wall and touches a picture.*]

RICHARD: Picture. Lots of pictures on that wall.

THOMASINA: Oh, yes [*touches two pictures*].

[*She touches another picture.*]

Oh, this is nice. It's very intricate. Is it carved?

RICHARD: No, it's not carved, it's moulded, but it is very pretty.

[*He walks on and up the futon to be with her.*]

THOMASINA: Is it a nice picture?

RICHARD: No, not particularly. But it is worth a hell of a lot more than any of the others.

THOMASINA: Oh, very nice.

[RICHARD *looks at the picture and straightens it while she moves along the edge of the bed.*]

Oh, I seem to have stepped on something . . .

RICHARD: Oh.

THOMASINA: I think it's sour underwear [*she laughs*].

RICHARD [*hurrying to pick up dirty clothes*]: Yes, some washing I meant to put away.

THOMASINA [*giggles*]: Are you very untidy?

RICHARD: Um, well, no, not more than . . .

[*He picks up other clothes and towels left lying around and jams them all into a drawer of the chest of drawers.*]

Er. Tom, would you like some coffee, tea . . . I think I even have some whisky if you prefer?

THOMASINA: I'd like some coffee, please.

RICHARD: Right, coffee, I'll just put the kettle on.

[*Goes into kitchen.*]

Please make yourself at home.

[*Takes off jacket and puts it over back of chair at the desk.*]

THOMASINA: Yes, thank you. [*Moves along front of bed, and finds chest of drawers. Investigates it*] Have you stripped this chest, Richard?

RICHARD [*coming out of kitchen holding coffee jar*]: Sorry?

THOMASINA: Have you stripped this?

RICHARD: Yeah. It's something I started a few years ago. Never did get round to finishing it.

THOMASINA [*continuing to feel it with her fingertips*]: Is it pine?

RICHARD: Yeah. Just ordinary pine.

[*She moves, and kicks tool-box.*]

Oh, sorry, that's my tool-box.

[*He closes and pushes tool-box away.*]

THOMASINA [*laughing*]: You keep having to put things away.

RICHARD: Yes!

[*He goes back into kitchen. She continues to investigate, going to the end of the chest*]

THOMASINA: Oh, this feels nice [*she has found a small cabinet on the table*].

RICHARD [*returning from kitchen*]: Yes, it is. I picked it up at an auction recently.

THOMASINA: It's very highly polished. What kind of wood is it?

RICHARD: Light mahogany. You see it has a couple of little drawers here, and underneath there are six compartments for, um, scrolls . . . sandwiches . . .

[*As she knocks over cereal packet on the table.*]

Oh, that's a Shredded Wheat packet . . . [*He goes to kitchen with packet and puts it away. He looks in fridge*] Er, Tom, I wonder if you'd mind having it black — I seem to have run out of milk?

THOMASINA: No.

RICHARD: Oh, good. Would you like to sit down?

THOMASINA [*a little embarrassed*]: Yes.

RICHARD: Over here, the armchair.

[*Leads her to it and puts her hand on the arm, taking some clothes off it at the same time. He goes back into kitchen. She sits down, and investigates the space to the front of the chair and then to the side, where she comes across a cardboard box. She smiles.*]

THOMASINA: I like that restaurant we went to, Richard. It felt very warm and cosy.

RICHARD [*coming back with the coffee*]: Yes, more than can be said for the waiter.

THOMASINA: Oh. I liked him.

RICHARD: One other thing, do you take sugar?

THOMASINA: No.

RICHARD: Good, because I haven't got any. [*Holding the cup in front of her for a moment — no response*] Er, it's here. And please be careful, it's very hot.

[*He gives her the coffee carefully and goes for his tobacco, which is in his jacket pocket on the chair by the table. She sips her coffee.*]

THOMASINA: I thought if you were a diabetic you needed to have sugar around all the time.

RICHARD: Not necessarily. You're thinking of the hypo emergencies. I keep some Devon toffees for those. Rather look forward to my emergencies, as a matter of fact. Er, Tom, would you like a roll-up?

THOMASINA: No, thank you, actually I've got some cigarettes in my bag, but I can't quite remember where I put it.

RICHARD: It's here. [*He hands bag to her from beside him on the bed and lights her cigarette*] Just give you a light. There we are. Oh, and one ashtray, on the little table beside you. [*He places an ashtray on the cardboard box*] So – here we are at last.

[*Takes shoes off, then rolls a cigarette. She smokes, and sips her coffee.*]

THOMASINA: I've just realized. You're not wearing your dark glasses tonight, are you?

RICHARD: No, I'm not.

THOMASINA: Does that mean the swelling has gone down?

RICHARD: Yes, that went down some time ago. I'm afraid the film star image went with it though.

THOMASINA: What about the car? Are you going to sell it?

RICHARD: No, I don't think so. I'll hang on to it for a bit, see how we get on.

THOMASINA: Is it legal to drive if you can only see with one eye?

RICHARD: I don't know. I hope so.

THOMASINA: And how's the toe? [*She is stroking the arm of the chair.*]

RICHARD: Toe?

THOMASINA: The toe!

RICHARD: Oh, the toe! I'd forgotten all about that. Yes, the toe's healed up completely now. Oh sorry, no pun intended! I just cut the nail straight across, as directed by the doctor, and it's been no problem.

THOMASINA: I meant to ask you actually. I know some diabetics lose sensitivity in their nerve-endings . . .

RICHARD: Yeh.

THOMASINA: Have you . . . Has it affected your playing the guitar?

RICHARD: No, I'm afraid not, I've always played like that.

[*They both laugh.*]

No, it's remained located in the feet.

THOMASINA: Well, one doesn't use one's feet for feeling much, does one? [*She is gently stroking the arm of the chair.*]

RICHARD: No no, that's true. Mind you, they say I'll never dance *Swan Lake* again. [*Pause*] You're incredibly sensitive, aren't you? I've noticed that about you, how tactile you are. You always like to feel the surfaces of things, like that armchair now.

[*Pause.*]

THOMASINA: I need to feel things. It's the way I know them, but I also like it.

RICHARD: Do you?

THOMASINA: I like the feel of this chair. It's very velvety.

RICHARD [*contemplating her hand and the chair*]: Velvety? Ah. Let me feel that.

[*He comes across and strokes the chair.*]

Oh, wow! that's amazing if you shut your eyes. It's quite different — it's like I've never felt that before.

THOMASINA: I think you've got very lazy about your sense of touch, Richard.

RICHARD [*not hearing her*]: Sorry?

THOMASINA [*she laughs*]: I said you've got very lazy about your sense of touch.

RICHARD [*laughing*]: Oh yes . . .

THOMASINA: And your hearing as well.

RICHARD: Oh, thank you very much. You're painting a picture of a decrepit over here.

[*She laughs.*]

I suppose you can hear through walls?

THOMASINA [*jokily*]: Well, as a matter of fact my auditory organs are highly efficacious.

[*They both laugh at that.*]

They certainly tell me an awful lot about you.

[*Puts cigarette out.*]

RICHARD: Oh, do they? And what do they tell you about me?

THOMASINA [*taking her time, and relishing her words*]: Well, that you are very sensitive ... you've got a wonderful sense of humour and I like the way you don't explain your jokes.

RICHARD: I don't think I could.

THOMASINA: And I like the low timbre of your voice. It's very sensual.

RICHARD [*in a very low register*]: Ah, yes.

THOMASINA: But my sense of you isn't just limited to what I hear.

RICHARD: Is it not?

THOMASINA: Oh, no. It's much more fulsome than that.

RICHARD: Really, how?

THOMASINA: I feel your presence, your warmth, I smell you ...

RICHARD [*interrupting*]: Oh, I smell as well now, do I?

THOMASINA: Oh, my olfactory sense of you is very full.

[*They are both amused at her choice of words.*]

RICHARD: Probably my olfactory socks.

THOMASINA [*she laughs*]: No, I don't mean that you're smelly. I mean that part of my perception of you is your very distinctive aroma.

RICHARD: Ah, I've got a distinctive aroma. Um, what's it like, this 'distinctive aroma'?

THOMASINA: Well [*choosing her words carefully*] it's sort of sharp ... pungent ... lingering ... with just a hint of sweat! It's very earthy!

RICHARD: Well, I'm glad it's just a hint.

THOMASINA: How do I smell to you?

RICHARD [*pauses*]: Well ... very nice.

[*They both laugh.*]

THOMASINA: Is that the best you can do, Richard?

RICHARD: I'm afraid my olfactory organs aren't as highly developed as yours. Tell me, is that anything to do with why you keep asking me to sit closer to you?

THOMASINA: No, that's more to do with concentration.

RICHARD: On what?

THOMASINA: On you.

RICHARD: On me?

THOMASINA: Well, the closer you are to me, the more I understand you.

RICHARD: I see. Well, look, I'd hate to be misunderstood. Would you like me to sit a little closer now?

THOMASINA: Mmm.

[*He moves and kneels on the floor by her chair.*]

RICHARD: Is this close enough?

THOMASINA: Yes.

RICHARD [*pauses*]: Tom, can I ask you a question? I know it may sound daft, but ... have you any idea of what I actually look like?

THOMASINA: Oh yes.

RICHARD: Have you? How?

THOMASINA: I asked Sue!

RICHARD [*he laughs*]: That's cheating!

THOMASINA: Why is it cheating? How else would I know?

RICHARD: Well, I don't know, I just didn't expect you to

say that you asked Sue. But supposing you weren't living with Sue, supposing there was nobody you could ask, would you still be able to form a visual image of me?

THOMASINA: No; but I've never considered that to be very important. What really matters is my sensation of you.

RICHARD: Ah. So, when you're talking to me, you don't have an image of me in your mind's eye?

THOMASINA: No. I have you. I sense you . . . You don't understand, do you?

RICHARD: Well . . .

THOMASINA: Well, if you like someone, you like them, their essence, what they really are . . . of course I'd like to see you, but I never will so I don't worry about it. I have you. I have a very complete sense of you.

RICHARD [*pauses*]: Well . . . I said it was a daft question.

[*His hand has been beside hers during this and they now start to delicately stroke finger-tips.*]

THOMASINA [*pauses*]: I'd like to know what your experience of me is.

RICHARD: My experience of you? Well. [*Pause*] I think you're very beautiful.

THOMASINA: Am I?

RICHARD: Yes, you are. I think you're very warm and

generous and sensitive. There's a great serenity about you. I like the way you hold your body, the way you turn your head into your shoulder sometimes, it's very . . . [*Pause*] it's very sensual.

[*Their fingers have been caressing more and more during this.*]

THOMASINA: And you don't mind that I'm blind?

RICHARD: No.

[*He kisses her fingers, and puts her fingers in his mouth. He gently touches her hair. They draw closer and hug each other very tightly.*]

God, I thought we'd never get here!

THOMASINA: It's been months.

RICHARD: [*Kissing her neck*]: You are very beautiful.

[*He caresses her face, neck and shoulders.*]

THOMASINA: Richard, there is something I'd like to do. You know I explained that the way that I know things is by touching them?

RICHARD: Mmm.

THOMASINA: Well, I'd like to know you; I'd like to take your clothes off and explore your body . . . Is that alright?

[*Pause.*]

RICHARD: Yes.

[*She takes his hand and positions him at the end of the bed, standing. She removes his shirt, trousers and underpants, socks. She strokes his face with her finger-tips.*]

THOMASINA: I think you are very beautiful ... soft skin. [*Touches shoulders and touches his chest*] You're so hairy! I didn't think you'd be hairy!

[*Pause.*]

RICHARD: I take after my mother.

THOMASINA [*laughs. She walks round him to explore his back, licks it, sniffs it, works her way down to his buttocks. She works her way down his legs, to his feet, explores his toes, comes back to face him. Explores his pubic hair and gently takes his penis between her fingers and touches it lightly. Takes his face in her hand*]: That will do nicely, thank you.

[*Black-out.*
Music: 'I want you', Abbey Road L.P. – Beatles.]

SCENE 2

A couple of weeks later.
Early morning, 7.30 a.m. RICHARD *sitting on bed, half-dressed,*
preparing to inject insulin.

Jane sitting up in bed reading 'Men Only'.

[*Pause.*]

JANE: Do you wank on this?

RICHARD: What?

JANE: Do you wank on this?

RICHARD: Well ... um ... why?

JANE: Pathetic.

[*He returns to preparing the syringe.*]

Is this what you do when I'm not here?

RICHARD: Yes ... yes ... That's why I'm going blind.

JANE: If you really wanted to discover yourself, you'd do it with real people not pictures. [*She throws magazine to the end of the bed.*]

RICHARD: Well, I only buy them for the crosswords. Now, which thigh gets it today?

JANE: I didn't sleep at all last night ...

RICHARD: The left one I think.

JANE: After we had screwed.

RICHARD [*he injects*]: And it's one hundred and eighty!

JANE: I said, I didn't sleep at all last night after we had screwed.

RICHARD: Oh, didn't you? I think I must have dropped off like a log. [*He throws needle into bin.*]

JANE: You always do.

RICHARD: I thought it was rather good last night, wasn't it?

JANE: Oh, it was alright as far as it went – it just didn't go far enough.

RICHARD: Oh! Well I do the best with what I've got, Jane.

[*He goes towards kitchen with syringe box and mug of tea.*]

JANE: It was just a fuck; you could have been fucking any-body.

[RICHARD *goes to kitchen, he puts box in bag and comes back with some bread.*]

RICHARD: Want some toast?

JANE: No.

[RICHARD *goes back to kitchen and puts toast in toaster.*]

There's no point in going to Portobello now, you've missed all the bargains anyway.

RICHARD: What?

JANE: I said you're too late for the bargains.

RICHARD: Oh probably ... But I've got to go. If I don't turn up this week, they're going to start thinking I'm just a punter – won't take me seriously.

JANE: Why do you never listen to anything I say?

[*Pause.*]

You look terrible; you could do with a rest.

RICHARD: I agree. But there you are; there's no rest for the wicked, or picture dealers.

JANE [*getting out of bed*]: If you don't look after yourself, you'll just fall apart; you won't be able to see at all soon if you're not careful.

RICHARD: Alright, Jane, thank you very much. I *was* awake at six, you know — wide awake. Just went back to sleep again. Why didn't you keep me awake?

JANE: Richard, I don't want you to go down to Portobello today; we need to talk.

RICHARD: What about?

JANE: About us.

RICHARD: Ah, right [*goes off to kitchen*].

JANE: Where are you going? Richard, for Christ's sake, I've just said we need to talk!

RICHARD: Just going to make the toast.

[*Jane puts trousers on.*]

RICHARD [*from kitchen*]: I can hear you quite well from here actually, Jane, if you want to, er . . .

[*She goes across to kitchen door.*]

JANE: I don't want to talk to you in the kitchen. I want you out here. I want your complete and undivided attention.

RICHARD: Won't be a minute. Just put the jam . . .

[*Pause.*]

JANE: Hurry up, Richard! For Christ's sake; you're so bloody slippery!

[RICHARD *puts marge and jam on and puts things away.*

*Comes back into room, picks up mug of tea from table and sits
on chair. He looks at toast, then at her.*]

RICHARD: I don't want this.

JANE: Richard, I am fed up with having a relationship where
we never see each other. You said it would be more or less
the same.

RICHARD: Umm, well, I don't think I ever said it would be
more or less the same.

JANE: You said it wouldn't make any difference if we
weren't living together.

RICHARD: I think what I actually said was that for a relationship to stay alive it has to change.

JANE: Look, I can put up with you wanting to live separately
from me. I understand that you don't want us to spend all
our time together. I don't mind if you want a chance to
find yourself. But I cannot stand this . . . this vagueness.

RICHARD: What do you mean 'vagueness'?

JANE: I don't know what's happening from one moment to
the next. I spend half my time on the phone trying to get
hold of you; and when I do manage to pin you down and
commit yourself to something, like Wednesday, I get a call
from you the night before to say 'terribly sorry, Jane —
can't make it'!

[*He puts down toast and picks up tobacco from chest of drawers
and rolls cigarette.*]

RICHARD: Ah, now come on, Jane, I did explain that that was very important business.

JANE: Richard, I am very important business! How about planning your life around me for a change! You know what I want, Richard: I want to feel that we're a unit, that we belong together. I don't want to be popping round here now and again. I hate sleeping in a strange bed. There's no space for me here; I don't feel comfortable.

RICHARD: Well, a futon does take some getting used to.

JANE [*sits on futon*]: Alright, Richard. If you want me to get used to it, I suggest that we spend three or four nights of the week together. That I have somewhere to keep my things. That we get organized about food so I don't have to keep worrying about you all the time. And that I have a front door key.

RICHARD: For Christ's sake, Jane, that would be just like living back together again.

JANE: No, it's not: I live in Hackney.

RICHARD: Well, you wouldn't be under that arrangement.

JANE [*moves to face* RICHARD]: If we have a relationship . . . do we have a relationship?

RICHARD: Erm, yes, of course we've got a relationship.

JANE: Then it has to be something more than an occasional Vindaloo!

RICHARD: Look, Jane, don't you think it's just a bit early to be discussing all this?

JANE: Richard, it's always too early for you to discuss anything you don't want to face up to.

[RICHARD *looks at watch.*]

I don't care what time it is. I want to get this sorted out now.

[RICHARD *reaches for his toast.*]

Sod your toast! I didn't sleep at all last night, worrying about what's happening to us! I'm fed up with being treated like a bloody whore! I want to feel that I'm important to you, that you care for me. I've got a home in Hackney and I want you to be there with me.

RICHARD: Well, I can't.

JANE: Why not?

RICHARD: I've moved out.

JANE: Then you've moved out of the relationship.

RICHARD: Erm, well, no – I don't see that that logically follows – I mean after all it's, er . . . well, it's only been a couple of weeks, hasn't it? I mean, don't you think we should just give it some time?

JANE: I know what will happen. I'll be the only one putting anything into this relationship. I've done my best to go along with what you want, but you're not making any effort at all. If we don't do something about it together, it's just going to fizzle out.

RICHARD: Erm, no, I don't see why it should, er . . . I mean . . . well . . . look – Jane, I think the best thing we can do is this. I'll shoot off to Portobello now, get the business done as quickly as possible and come straight back. [*He is moving away to get his jacket*] In the meantime I think you should go back to bed and get a few hours' kip because obviously you're over-tired, and then we can both get down to discussing everything that needs to be discussed – that's a promise!

JANE [*gets up and moves to* RICHARD]: No, I don't want you to go. If we don't sort this out now . . .

RICHARD: Jane, I've got to go.

[*She holds on to his jacket. The situation very quickly develops into an argument and struggle for the coat until* RICHARD pulls the coat from her angrily.]

JANE [*picks up the 'Men Only' and throws it at him with great force*]: Sod your pornographic magazine! [*Picks up pillows, and throws them*] Sod your pillows, Sod your Portobello Road! [*She looks around for something else to throw as* RICHARD *stands protecting himself, gaping. She sees mattress, grabs it and with all her strength drags it into the middle of the room, screaming as she moves*] Sod your bloody futon!!! [*And breaks down, collapses into it. Sobbing heavily.*]

[*Pause.*]

RICHARD [*moving towards her, tentatively touching her head gently*]: I'm sorry.

JANE: Oh, sod off!!!

RICHARD: For Christ's sake!

[*He rushes out of the room.* JANE *continues sobbing.*

Fast fade to blackout.

Music: 'We can work it out' — Beatles.]

SCENE 3

A month or so later.

Lights up. THOMASINA *enters, with white cane.*

THOMASINA: Richard, the front door was open. [*Stops*] Richard? [*Puts cane and bag in chair – goes to the bed, investigates*] Richard? [*Stands up*] Richard, are you in the kitchen?

RICHARD [*opening the kitchen door quickly*]: Tom? Where are you?

THOMASINA: I'm here.

[*They find each other and clutch tightly.*]

RICHARD: Where the hell have you been?

THOMASINA: I've been ringing you and ringing you. I didn't know where you were.

RICHARD: I didn't know ... I ...

[*They slowly break the embrace. She touches his shoulders.*]

Shall I take your coat? [*moment of slight embarrassment.*]

[*He goes and hangs it over a chair.*]

Please sit down if you, er . . .

[*She sits on chair.*]

THOMASINA: So what happened?

RICHARD: Well, as I said on the phone, the other eye haemorrhaged and, er – that was that.

THOMASINA: Where were you?

RICHARD: I was at an auction – Phillips – I'd gone to bid for some pictures. [*He sits on bed.*] Lot twelve was my first bid, and just as they got to lot eleven it went – just like that.

THOMASINA: What, just immediately?

RICHARD: Well, yes, it was like a curtain coming down. [*Pause*] The extraordinary thing is that the only thought I had in my mind was, how the hell am I going to bid for the next lot? That's all I could think, how the hell am I going to . . .

[*Pause.*]

THOMASINA: What did you do?

RICHARD: Well, I just bid for it. Actually I don't know

whether I got it or not. Damn, I must find out about that. Yes . . .

[*Pause.*]

THOMASINA: Go on.

RICHARD: Well, after a while I began to think, er . . . this is ridiculous, I must do something about this. So I found my way downstairs to reception and, er, asked one of the girls to get me a taxi. [*Pause*] I remember putting my hands in my pocket because I thought that would look very normal and natural, as if nothing had happened. [*Pause.*]

[THOMASINA *overtly reacts to this and looks away from him.*]

I was standing beside the cab and I heard the cab driver saying, 'Where do you want to go guv, where do you want to go?' He kept repeating it. 'Where do you want to go. Where do you want to . . .' And do you know what? I had absolutely no idea of where I should . . . I didn't know where I could . . . [*Pause*] Anyway, I heard myself say Moorfields Eye Hospital and he took me there. [*Pause*] In the out-patients department, the girl at reception said, 'Can I help you?' I said, 'Yes I hope so – I've, er, lost my sight.' 'Oh yes,' she said, 'and do you have an appointment?'

[THOMASINA *turns to look at him.*]

I said, 'Well, no, I didn't know I was going to lose it.' It all seemed so bizarre.

THOMASINA: So what then?

RICHARD: Well, after God knows how long, I was eventually taken upstairs and everybody was looking and poking around . . . and people kept coming up to me and talking to me as if they knew me, 'Hello, Richard.' I hadn't a clue who they were. Anyway, eventually a nurse bunged me in a bed, slapped an ice pack on my eyes, and said, 'Right, your forty-eight-hour rest period starts as of – now!'

[*Pause.*]

THOMASINA: How did you get back here?

RICHARD: One of your mob brought me back, the social worker. He came in for a while. Said he wanted to check that there were no dangers or hazards for me. Gave me a conducted tour of my own room. Showed me where the tea and coffee was.

THOMASINA: When is he coming back?

RICHARD: I don't know . . . he didn't . . . I don't know.

THOMASINA: Didn't he make any arrangements?

RICHARD: No, no, he didn't . . . no . . . Oh yes, I'm getting a Home Help. A Home Help! Twice a week to do a bit of shopping, tidy up, washing. [*Pause*] Always wanted an 'au pair'.

[*Pause.*]

THOMASINA: Did they say how long?

RICHARD: For what?

THOMASINA: For the blood to clear.

RICHARD: Oh no, no – they didn't say anything. No, *nothing* as usual. But I know it could take anything up to three months.

THOMASINA: And they can't do anything until then?

RICHARD: No, nothing.

THOMASINA: Can you see anything at all now?

RICHARD: Not really, just some light and dark. Some light over there. Must be the street light.

THOMASINA [*pauses*]: Did anyone come to see you?

RICHARD: Where?

THOMASINA: In hospital.

RICHARD: Oh yes, Harvey called in in the morning, and Jane called in in the evening.

THOMASINA: How did she know?

RICHARD: Erm. She phoned the gallery about something and Oscar told her what had happened so she just called in to, um . . . er, she just called in. [*Pause*] Good bloke Harvey, damned good bloke. [*Pause*] Tom?

THOMASINA: Yes.

RICHARD: Glad you're here.

[*She moves across to him and sits on the bed with him and strokes his head.*]

THOMASINA: I wish I'd seen you in hospital, you've been going through all this and I just wasn't there.

RICHARD: Well, you'll just have to make up for it now, won't you? [*Pause*] Would you like a whisky?

THOMASINA: Yes – [*surprised*] alright.

RICHARD: Good. Let's get pissed. Let's get sloshed, shall we? [*He gropes to the Georgian bookcase to find whisky, knocking things over and cursing*] There was a bookcase over here somewhere. Ah, here it is. *He opens bookcase – tins fall to floor*] Bugger!

THOMASINA: Are you all right?

RICHARD: Yeah, fine. Ah-ha, whisky! Now two glasses.

[*There is a minute amount in the bottle. He pours it all into one glass.*]

Oh! damn!

THOMASINA: What's the matter?

RICHARD: Look, Tom, do you mind if we just have it in one glass, there really isn't enough for two.

THOMASINA: No, we'll share it.

[*He gropes his way to the futon, where she is now sitting.*]

Richard, what about your injections?

RICHARD: Injections. Oh, I've given those up.

THOMASINA: You mean you haven't injected for two days?

RICHARD: That was a joke. No, they've given me a pre-set syringe so I don't have to, er – think. Here, first snort to you.

[*Sitting next to her. Pause.*]

Oh God, what must we look like?

[*Pause.*]

THOMASINA: What do you think we look like?

[*Pause.*]

RICHARD: Mmm?

[*Pause.*]

THOMASINA: Do you want some of this?

RICHARD: Ah, thank you, cheers [*drinks*]. Here, hold this and don't go away, I'll be right back.

THOMASINA: Where are you going?

RICHARD: To get my tobacco. Should be ... [*He gets it from the cardboard box and returns to bed. Opens the tin and fumbles about*] Oh damn! Where the hell have they gone?! Ah, I know. You've got to have a good memory in this game. Ah, got them! (*Pause*) Oh damn!

THOMASINA: What's wrong?

RICHARD: Lost my papers.

THOMASINA: Where did you last have them?

RICHARD: I don't know, I'll just have to go and look for them.

[*He goes.*]

THOMASINA: Where are they usually?

RICHARD: They're not usually anywhere, they're just there! Ah-ha! found them! First time.

[*He has found them on the floor by the cardboard box.*]

THOMASINA: Pretty impressive. I think you've been having secret lessons.

[*He sits next to her and starts to roll cigarette. Pause.*]

RICHARD: Radio 4 can be oppressive, you know. I always used to enjoy it, but I had fifteen hours of it on the trot yesterday.

THOMASINA: It would get a bit boring.

RICHARD: There's bugger-all else to do.

THOMASINA: I feel really inadequate, Richard. I feel as if I should be able to help in some way. But I don't know how to . . . I can't even imagine what it could be like . . .

RICHARD [*cursing under his breath*]: I'll have given up smoking by the time I get this damn thing rolled. Oh, that'll have to do, whatever it looks like.

[*He carefully licks paper, screws it up and throws it away with a curse.*]

THOMASINA: What is it?

RICHARD: Oh, nothing. Just got the paper the wrong way round. [*Puts away tin.*]

THOMASINA: I've got some cigarettes in my bag, actually.

RICHARD: What are they, *Marlboro*? [*Exaggerating phonetics of 'Marlboro'.*]

THOMASINA: Yes.

RICHARD: Can't smoke *Marlboro* [*as above*]. Oh God, I'm sorry about all this. [*Pause*] I feel so damned useless.

[*She puts her arm around his. Pause. He laughs.*]

Crazy things that go through your mind. I even found myself talking to God again while I was in there. [*He laughs*] I said, 'God, excuse me. I know we haven't been in correspondence for some time now, but, er, we've got a slight problem down here and I was wondering that, erm, if I promised to give up being an atheist do you think you could do a quick miracle on the side?' [*Pause*] I don't think she was listening. What shall we do now?

THOMASINA: We'll do what we usually do.

RICHARD: What do we usually do?

THOMASINA: Well, we'd listen to the radio or we'd have something to eat, or we'd go to bed and make love, or we'd just lark about and be silly . . . we can still do any of those.

RICHARD [*pauses*]: Yes.

[*Pause.*]

Shall we dance!? We've never danced together, have we? Would you like to?

THOMASINA: I'm not very good at dancing.

RICHARD: That's alright, neither am I. [*He gets up and moves to where he thinks the record player is*] However, there's just one proviso: you'll have to dance to anything that comes up because I haven't a clue what order the records are in. [*He finds himself at the clothes-rack*] Where the hell am I?

THOMASINA: It's over here.

[*She crosses to stereo and raises lid. He collects himself.*]

RICHARD: Yup, OK, right, I've got it, thank you. Now, I'll take the first record in the pile and whatever it is we dance to it, OK?

THOMASINA: Alright.

RICHARD: Even Stravinsky? [*Trying to put record on deck*] How the hell do you find the hole? Ah!

[*It is 'Come Together' from Abbey Road L.P. He plays it very loud.*]

Les Beatles!

THOMASINA: Richard, it's too loud!

[*They dance together, THOMASINA very nervously. RICHARD does a whirl, loses balance, falls down, it frightens him, he scrambles to the bed. THOMASINA turns off music and joins him on bed.*]

RICHARD: I'm sorry – it's alright. I just . . . Oh God!

THOMASINA: Are you alright? Did you hurt yourself?

RICHARD: Just for a moment I was totally disorientated . . .

[*They hug each other tightly.*]

Damn, damn!

[THOMASINA *kisses his face. They become more and more passionate. They begin to tear each other's clothes off.* RICHARD *throws* THOMASINA *down on bed, pulling up her skirt and pulling at her tights and panties. She is pushing down his trousers.*]

RICHARD [*stopping suddenly and pulling away*]: NO!! I'm sorry, I'm sorry. It's alright, sorry.

[*He tries to find the right thing to say as he fumbles with his clothing. He leans against the chest of drawers beside the bed.*]

[*Whispered*] Damn, damn!

THOMASINA [*sitting up, jumper off, skirt up, tights pulled down*]: It doesn't matter . . . It's not important . . . Where are you?

[*Raises her arm towards him; he half stretches his arm towards her. Their hands do not meet as the lights slowly fade.*

Music: 'One Day (At a Time)', Mind Games L.P. – John Lennon.]

SCENE 4

A few weeks later.
Evening.

There are no lights on in RICHARD'*s room.*
Quite loud music is playing on the hi-fi – Lennon 'One Day (At a Time)'.

RICHARD *enters in the dark, smoking a cigarette, and crosses to the hi-fi.* JANE *follows, with difficulty, calling out to him from the passage. As she enters, she puts on the light.*

JANE: It's about time you got some light bulbs in the hall.

[*She removes coat etc. and hangs on hook.*]

RICHARD: Oh, really.

JANE: I've, er, brought a bottle of wine for us.

RICHARD: Ah, good.

JANE: I had a bit of quiche in the fridge; I thought you might like it for your lunch tomorrow.

RICHARD: Thank you; I think I'll have it now.

JANE: Haven't you eaten yet?

RICHARD: No, not yet.

JANE: It's after half past eight, Richard.

RICHARD: Is it really? Good Lord, doesn't time fly when you're enjoying yourself!

JANE: I'll heat it up.

RICHARD: No, I'll have it cold. [*He picks up syringe box*] Just jack up first, alright?

[JANE *goes into kitchen.* RICHARD *prepares to inject.*]

JANE [*returning*]: Your quiche is on the table, and the wine.

RICHARD: Thank you.

JANE: Isn't it rather dangerous doing that by yourself?

RICHARD: Well, yes. I normally invite a crowd of friends round to watch, but I put them off tonight.

JANE: But how can you be sure how much insulin you've got in?

RICHARD: Well, you see, inside the bottle there's a little man, and when there's enough he taps on the side.

JANE: Yes, but you can't tell if all the bubbles have gone.

RICHARD: No. One bubble and he was dead.

[JANE *starts to tidy bed etc.*]

JANE: Sorry I was a bit late coming round; I had rather a lot of mounting to do.

RICHARD: Oh yes? [*Pause*] Anyone I know?

JANE: Is your Home Help still coming?

RICHARD: My 'au pair'? Yes.

JANE: Is it still the black lady?

RICHARD: Yes, still black.

JANE: Have you found out her name yet?

RICHARD: No. I call her Bertha.

[*He throws needle towards the bin. She goes to pick it up.*]

JANE: [*taking a shirt across to the clothes-rack*]: What has happened to the Guillman?

RICHARD: The Guillman.

JANE: Yes, the little man on the bridge.

RICHARD: Yes, I know what the Guillman is.

JANE: Well, where is it?

RICHARD: Gone to auction.

JANE: What for?

RICHARD: Well, it seemed like a good idea to the bank manager and the VAT man.

JANE [*sitting on bed*]: Did anything come of that icon you mentioned to me?

RICHARD: I don't know. Oscar's dealing with it for me; with any luck the Yanks'll buy it.

JANE: If I can ... I mean, things must be a bit difficult for you at the moment, so if I can help out at all ...

RICHARD: What do you mean?

JANE: Well, if you need any financial assistance, I, er ...

RICHARD: Oh, money.

JANE: Well, you've only got to ask.

RICHARD: Thank you.

JANE: Well, the wine should have breathed enough by now.

RICHARD: I should think it's gasping.

JANE: Only 'el cheapo' from the local offy, I'm afraid.

RICHARD: Scrummy.

JANE: Makes things go smoothly.

RICHARD: Yes.

[JANE *hands* RICHARD *the wine.*]

RICHARD: Thank you. Cheers.

JANE: Cheers, Richard. [*Pause*]. Shall I put some music on? [*She goes across to stereo system*] I think too much John Lennon is a bit depressing. Have you managed to keep your records sorted?

RICHARD: I try. Jane? [*Moves to middle of room*] Come here a minute.

JANE [*joining him*]: What?

RICHARD: Do you want to hear a joke?

JANE: Yes, alright.

RICHARD: Have you got your glasses on?

JANE: Of course I've got my glasses on.

RICHARD: Could you take them off?

JANE: Glasses off. Ready for action.

RICHARD [*during the joke he feels the contours of her face, the way blind people are 'supposed' to do, finishing up at her mouth*]: Well, you see, this blind man goes up to a bar and says to the man behind the counter: 'Excuse me, are you the barman?' 'Yer, what do you want?' 'Well, I'm awfully sorry to bother you, but do you know there's no paper in your lavatory?' [*He steps back and chuckles.*]

JANE: I don't think that's very funny. Your fingers stink of quiche! How about a little Mozart – in G Minor. I do prefer the minor keys; they always seem to come at you sideways.

   [*She puts on Mozart's string quartet in D Major, side 2, 1st*

Movement — Amadeus Quartet, Deutsche Gramaphone.
RICHARD *slumps in armchair.*]

This is nice and cosy. [*She puts the side lights on, turns main lights off and sits on bed*] What have you been up to recently?

RICHARD: Um, well, keeping busy. [*Pause*] Went train-spotting last week.

JANE: You've forgotten your wine [*collects it from chest of drawers*].

RICHARD: Thank you.

JANE: [*pauses*] Are you alright?

RICHARD: Mmm.

JANE: You seem very quiet.

RICHARD: Do I? Sorry.

JANE: I thought you weren't going to let me come round tonight. You didn't sound very keen on the phone.

RICHARD: Really? Well, never mind, you're here now. So what did you want to say?

JANE: Well, it was really going back to what you said last week. For some reason I've been bothered by it. I know we've said a lot to each other in the past . . .

RICHARD: Jane? I wonder if you'd mind turning that music off.

JANE: I've only just put it on.

RICHARD: Yes; it's just a little difficult to listen to two things at once.

JANE: I thought it would be easier; I thought your hearing became more sensitive when . . . well, when you couldn't see. You never used to find music a distraction. Is that better?

RICHARD: Thank you. You were saying?

JANE: Well, one or two of the things you said to me have rather hung around. It's not that I'm oversensitive, but I've been terribly conscious of the way I talk, the way I look. I've been going round school all week looking in mirrors, checking up.

RICHARD: Oh yes; and what did you see?

JANE: Oh, just a few more grey hairs. So rather than ignore it or get angry with you about it, I thought it would be better to come and talk with you and see if I could get it clear that way. You see, I've never thought of myself as being . . . well . . . 'tight-lipped', and I thought it might be you projecting some of your resentment on to me. Do you understand what I'm talking about?

RICHARD: Go on.

JANE: Well, haven't you anything to say about it?

RICHARD: No.

JANE: Did you mean what you said?

RICHARD: Yes.

JANE: Well, what exactly did you mean by what you said?

RICHARD: I meant exactly what I said.

JANE: Well, that's just not good enough. I think I'm very open. But obviously it's very difficult to be totally objective about oneself; and if you can see something about me that I can't, then I want to know about it. How do you feel about that?

RICHARD [*gestures*]: I . . .

JANE: Well, haven't you got anything to say?

RICHARD: No.

JANE: You're impossible. It's a waste of time coming round here. You refuse to make any effort to meet me halfway.

RICHARD: Jane, let's cut the crap, shall we? Why don't we just get pissed and watch telly?

JANE: Isn't that just typical of you, Richard? You've spent the whole of your life avoiding what is going on around you . . . You just completely opt out.

RICHARD: Yes, I suppose I do. I never really saw the advantage of it before.

JANE: So you've finally admitted it. And God has taken away your sight to make it easier for you. Aren't you lucky! [*Pause*] Sorry. I'm sorry that was a bit over the top. I am sorry. Deep breath, Jane; back to the beginning.

   [*Pause.* RICHARD *gets up and moves to the desk.*]

Can I help?

RICHARD: No, it's alright. Yes: you can find my cigarettes for me.

JANE: They're by the record player.

[RICHARD *moves towards the record player while* JANE *presents him with them, not knowing quite what to do. He is still feeling around when she places it in his hand.*]

RICHARD: Thank you.

[*She hands the matches to him.*]

JANE: Matches.

[*Shakes the box near his face.*]

RICHARD [*taking matches and shaking them also*]: So they are.

[RICHARD *sits again.* JANE *gets ashtray.* RICHARD *takes cigarette out and is about to light it.*]

JANE: The ashtray's by your cardboard box. [*She sits on arm of chair and hugs him*] I do think you're being very brave.

RICHARD: Sorry?

JANE: I said I think you're being very brave.

RICHARD: What about?

JANE: About not being able to see, of course.

RICHARD: Oh, that.

JANE: If it was me, I'd be curled up in a heap on the floor.

RICHARD: Would you? How do *you* know? [*Pause*]

Bravery's got bugger all to do with it actually. Bravery implies that there's some sort of choice; I've got no choice.

JANE: You've got a choice in how you deal with it; it seems to me you're dealing with it bravely.

RICHARD: But it doesn't matter whether I deal with it bravely or like a jibbering coward. I still pee on the floor; I still lose the damned cigarettes.

[JANE *moves back to the bed.*]

Jane, all I'm trying to do is get through this with as few burns and bruises as possible. I don't walk around the flat 'being brave'. Let me tell you, when I came out of hospital last week I was scared shitless. And don't tell me it's just temporary; I know it's just temporary, but the fact remains that I am B-L-I-N-D, blind! And I don't like it! [*Pause*] So, if you want to see all this as bravery, fine, you have it; but just don't patronize me with it.

JANE: I'm not patronizing you! I'm sorry I said it. I meant it at the time. I happen to think you are very brave. [*Pause*] Why do there always have to be these barriers between us?

RICHARD: They've kept us together, haven't they?

JANE: They drove us apart!

RICHARD: But you're here, aren't you?

JANE: Only just.

RICHARD: Why are you here, Jane?

[*She tries to respond, but is unable to get the words out.*]

Let's put it this way: why are we here . . .

JANE: God knows!

RICHARD: . . . together?

JANE: I don't know why I'm here, Richard. Hand of Fate brought me.

RICHARD: Hand of . . . for Christ's sake!

JANE: I do the best I can. I don't sit around all day wondering why I am here.

RICHARD: For Christ's sake, Jane, I'm not talking about the meaning of life. I'm talking about you and me, us, this room, here, together, now — why?

JANE: I'm here because after a great deal of difficulty I managed to persuade you to let me come round; and you are here because you live here.

RICHARD: No, no, no, no. Why are *we* here, together, now, this room — why?

JANE: Because I want to talk to you!

RICHARD: But, Jane, I have nothing to tell you. I have nothing to say. I've got no answers. I don't even have any questions. If you wanted to talk, you'd have done better to talk to your Women's Group or even the damned rabbit.

JANE: I've never had an intimate relationship with Henry.

RICHARD: That's not what Henry told me [*laughs*].

JANE: I am trying to be serious about this. Richard. There was a time when there was some love between us, and I thought, on the basis of that, I might be able to discover something about myself.

RICHARD: Jane, everything I had to say I said last week. I said it all last week.

JANE: But that's not enough. You can't just throw shit over me and leave it. You've got to wipe it off!

RICHARD: No; *you've* got to wipe it off!

JANE: You threw it!

RICHARD: It was your shit!

JANE: Maybe it's not my shit, maybe it's your shit, maybe it's all the rubbish inside of you you can't face up to, so you dump it on Jane.

RICHARD: Jane, what I said last week was the truth as I saw it. What you want me to do is explain it for you; well, I can't. As soon as you try to explain the truth, you start to lie about it. And I'm not going to do that –

JANE [*cutting it*]: Oh, what rubbish! The truth does not end with you saying to me that I have got tight lips and shrivelled tits.

RICHARD: I didn't mean that you literally had tight lips or shrivelled tits; it was meant metaphorically.

JANE: Let's not deal in semantics. The sentiment's the same.

RICHARD: No, it's not – it's quite the reverse. There's a degree of hope in my metaphor.

JANE: Thanks very much!

RICHARD: To say that you literally had shrivelled tits would have been offensive and I had no intention of being offensive . . .

JANE [*overlapping*]: It seems to me more likely that you're the one that's shrivelling.

RICHARD: What I was trying to explain was not that your tits were shrivelled but that's the way I see you going as a person, it was an image –

JANE [*cutting in*]: Stop talking so much rubbish! Stop avoiding the issue; take responsibility for what you said.

RICHARD: My responsibility lay in telling the truth as I saw it. I exercised that responsibility last week. I can do no more.

JANE: Oh, you sound so wonderfully pious.

RICHARD: Do I? Sound wonderfully pious, do I? Well it didn't sound pious to me, it sounded to me like I was trying to explain what I meant. But you thought it was pious. Thanks. [*Turning around addressing something behind him as he asks the question*] Did you think that was pious?

JANE: What? What you just said?

RICHARD: Did you think that was pious?

JANE: Conferring with your guardian angels, are you? Do they support you in this fantasy world?

RICHARD: I was just asking the bookcase and the door if they thought it was pious. They didn't think it was pious, I didn't think it was pious. So where does that leave us?

JANE: It leaves us where it always leaves us, with you refusing to face up to what is going on in front of you. Like you've always refused to deal with anything. You refuse to look after your body. You refuse to take any responsibility for your relationships. You just live in a dream world Richard, etc., etc., etc.

[RICHARD *screams loud and long. A long pause.*]

I'm sorry. I didn't mean to upset you. I, um, did think that we might have been able to talk for once.

[*Pause.*]

Suppose I'd better be going. I do try to understand you. It's just not very easy.

[*She hesitates.*]

I saw Duncan at the weekend. He said that he couldn't get any dope at the moment. But he rolled a joint for you. I'll put it by the television. Best of luck at the hospital. I hope all goes well with your appointment. I *am* sorry, Richard.

[*She is, by this time, very upset, barely able to control her anguish.*]

[*As* JANE *leaves,* RICHARD *starts to go into a hypo. He controls it until after she has left. He staggers to the desk and finds the quiche. He stuffs it into his mouth, forcing himself to eat. He spits it out, but has to pick it up and eat it again. He goes scrabbling about for his glass of wine, still trying to eat. He drinks and makes his way back to the desk, where he dumps the food. He searches for his bag and brings out a toffee. He is shaking considerably and it is difficult for him to unwrap the sweet. He eventually crams it in his mouth and sucks furiously. He slowly calms down, but as he does so he breaks down in tears. He makes himself stop, swigs from the bottle of wine and makes his way to the record player. He puts on the first record, which is 'Gimme Some Truth' by Lennon. He dances energetically. Gradually the emotion comes up for him again until he is dancing furiously and crying miserably. He beats his body and punches his face until he forces himself to stop. He quickly turns off the music and remains for a moment panting and scared. Emotion rises in him once more, which he tries to jam down but with little success. He scrambles for the bed and buries himself under the bedclothes.*

Fast fade to black-out. Pause.

Music: 'Just Because', Rock and Roll L.P. – John Lennon.]

SCENE 5

A few months later.

THOMASINA is sitting on the futon. RICHARD is standing and wearing a woolly hat and headphones round his neck; Lennon's 'Just Because' plays on his stereo system. RICHARD lights his cigarette and shakes the matchbox. THOMASINA takes the matches and lights her own cigarette. RICHARD sings along to the record.

RICHARD: Bye, John. [*Sings along; song ends*] Good track, that.

THOMASINA: Who is it?

RICHARD: It's John! John saying goodbye. [*Pause*] So, what's been happening in your neck of the woods this week?

THOMASINA: Well, I've been to work every day.

RICHARD: Every day? Any good abortions or suicides this week?

THOMASINA: No. A lot of people not being able to sign on because they were in hospital.

RICHARD: Oh dear.

THOMASINA: Quite ordinary things really.

RICHARD: Mmm.

[Pause.]

THOMASINA: Has Bertha been?

RICHARD: Yup; came yesterday.

THOMASINA: Have you seen Harvey this week?

RICHARD: Nope. [Pause] Saw the social worker Monday.

THOMASINA: Yes, you said on the phone.

RICHARD: Yep. Came to explain this BD8 form to me.

THOMASINA: Yes.

RICHARD: He said once that's filled in, then I would be registered officially and permanently blind. All this [pointing to his eyes] has been unofficial up to now, you see. He said I could get £1.25 off my television licence. Said I could apply for a white cane. I said I didn't mind having a white cane, but does it come in any other colours? [He laughs] Oh, and he said I could apply for a guide dog as well. Yes, wouldn't mind a guide dog [slight pause] so long as it was a Jack Russell. Do you think they train Jack Russells to be guide dogs?

THOMASINA: I don't think so, no.

RICHARD: Well, I'm not interested then. [*Pause*] So why did you want to come round?

THOMASINA: Because there are some things that I have to say.

RICHARD: About – us!

THOMASINA: Yes.

RICHARD: Da-da-a . . . Well?

THOMASINA: Well . . . I've been . . .

RICHARD: Hm?

THOMASINA: I've been . . . trying . . . to . . .

RICHARD: Could you speak up a little, Thomasina? It's very difficult to hear you.

THOMASINA: Yes, I'm sorry, I'm sorry. [*Pause*] I don't know where to start.

RICHARD: That's what they all say. When anyone starts with 'I don't know where to start', it usually means they don't know where to end. [*Pause. Sits on the floor*] Is that it, then?

THOMASINA: No . . . I've made an awful mess, Richard.

RICHARD: Oh dear.

THOMASINA: I should never have got involved with you in the first place; I should have found out more about diabetes . . . and I certainly shouldn't have started to have a sexual affair with you when I knew there was a problem with your eyes.

[RICHARD *puts headphones near chair . . . lots of noise.*]

I feel very responsible for the situation. You see, all my life I've been taught . . . well, it's just folly to get involved with someone who can't see . . . the only way to be alright as a blind woman is to be with someone who is sighted.

[RICHARD *crawls across floor looking for ashtray.*]

RICHARD: Excuse me. Is the ashtray here?

THOMASINA: Yes, it's here.

RICHARD: Thank you. Sorry, I interrupted you. You were saying something about how you were trained to take advantage of sighted men?

THOMASINA: That's not what I was saying.

RICHARD: Oh, sorry.

[*Pause.*]

Go on.

THOMASINA: I'm very sorry . . . I shouldn't have let it go on, but . . . I wanted you and it was so good, I just hoped you'd get your sight back and it would be alright.

RICHARD: Yes, well, apart from all that crap, what did you really want to say?

THOMASINA: I think it's impossible ... Richard ... It's impossible for me ...

RICHARD: So what you really wanted to say was: 'Richard, it's over, finished, goodbye.' There you are – simple, it's alright. I understand – you just don't go out with blind boys. I'm sure I wouldn't.

THOMASINA: That's not what it's about. It's about what you want from a relationship.

RICHARD: Oh yes? And do you know what you wanted from the relationship?

THOMASINA: Well, I think I know now, yes.

RICHARD: And what was that?

THOMASINA: I think ... I think ... I think I wanted to marry you and have children [*trying to control her grief*].

[*Pause.*]

RICHARD: Yup. But all that changed just like that last weekend when we found out that this was permanent?

THOMASINA: No, I've been thinking about it for some time, but I thought you had enough on your plate without my worries as well.

RICHARD: Just a minute. What do you mean you've been

thinking about it for some time? How long have you been thinking like this?

THOMASINA: Well, I suppose I've been worrying about it, well, since your other eye went really.

RICHARD: Oh. I see. Terrific! Thank you. So for the past couple of months while I've been thinking we've been having a wonderful and happy time, you were lying there thinking, 'What an impossible relationship'?

THOMASINA: No, it's not like that.

RICHARD: Well, what, then?!

THOMASINA: I never said it hasn't been wonderful for me too, but these things have been on my mind, yes.

RICHARD: But you couldn't say anything, could you?

THOMASINA: I couldn't . . . I couldn't . . . Richard. I get it very clear when I am away from you . . . but when I come back here and we're together in this room, what I'm thinking just seems to be unthinkable . . . here, where we've been so happy.

RICHARD: I see. So in this room it's all wonderful and happy; we walk through that door and suddenly it's impossible.

THOMASINA: No, not exactly.

RICHARD: Well, what the hell do you mean?!

THOMASINA: What I'm trying to say, Richard, is ... in here it's unreal ... out there there are ... people ...

RICHARD: What do you mean 'unreal'? This is my room.

THOMASINA: Oh, Richard, Richard! You seem to think being blind is about knocking your coffee over, or stubbing your toe on the end of the bed. You have no idea yet of what it's going to be like.

RICHARD: No. I realize of course that you have a head start on me, but I think I'm catching up pretty fast.

THOMASINA: You're going to go through such pain ... and I just can't bear to watch.

RICHARD: Pain! What do you mean 'pain'! How can you know I'll go through any pain?

THOMASINA: Because I've been through it! ... I'm frightened to be reminded of what I was like when I ... I've pretended it's easy because I wanted to impress you ... It's one thing being an interesting blind woman ... It's quite different when ... It's no good, Richard. There's no future for us as a blind couple.

RICHARD: We've been a blind couple for the past two months. What difference now?

THOMASINA: What kind of a life do you think we'd have ... We couldn't even go away on our own together, Richard, without someone having to take us to the toilet.

RICHARD: *What?*

[RICHARD's *lines are spoken over* THOMASINA's *in this speech.*]

THOMASINA: And what if we had children? How would we look after them? If they ran away in the park, who's going to fetch them back? You, with your white cane? –

RICHARD [*interrupting*]: I don't believe what I'm hearing here –

THOMASINA [*carrying on*]: We couldn't even keep a home clean, Richard, and no one would tell us if it was dirty because no one tells blind people stuff like that –

RICHARD [*again interrupting*]: We'll get someone in to clean –

THOMASINA: And what about me? Who is going to take me seriously in my job if I don't know what clothes I'm putting on in the morning? If I'm walking about the street with blood all over my skirt because I don't know that my period has started? I'd look like a stupid dirty blind woman! It would destroy us, Richard, don't you see. We'd drag each other down. All our sighted friends would disappear. We'd end up stuck with blind people all the time. Blind people are . . . boring!

RICHARD: Who says we have to be stuck with blind people all the time?

THOMASINA: Because that's what society does. It lumps you all together if you're a blind couple, that's all you are: You're BLIND!

RICHARD: Well, fuck society! I'm more than that! I'm more

than just blind! I'm still me! I'm still the same person you met and wanted six months ago. The only difference is I happen to have lost my sight, that's all. You're rejecting me because all your upbringing tells you that when a blind man comes along, you walk in the opposite direction; if he's sighted, you grab him! You hang on to him, you use him. Well, was that all you wanted when you met me, my eyes? Was that all?

THOMASINA: I don't know, I don't know.

RICHARD: No, you don't know because you're a stupid silly blind woman. You're not just blind, you can't perceive anything. You're blind from the inside out. You can't see me. You're not seeing me. All you're seeing is my blindness. It doesn't matter to you what a person is like, as long as they are sighted. That's all you care about, eyes, eyes, eyes. You're obsessed with eyes, eyes, eyes ...

THOMASINA: Yes, I want a sighted man, yes, it makes my life easier!

RICHARD: But you want more than that though, don't you? What you really want is to see, that's what you really want, isn't it? You want to see! You want to see! Don't you? Don't you? Go on, say it, say it! You want to see! Don't you? Don't you? [*He is standing over her, shaking her.*]

THOMASINA [*screaming*]: Yes, yes, I want to see! Yes, I want to see!

RICHARD: Well, you never will! You can't! How could you! You haven't even got your own eyes, they're false ... they're made of plastic, for Christ's sake ...

[THOMASINA *screams and covers her eyes during this.* RICHARD *throws her on the floor, screaming, into her ears.*]

You're a freak ... You're a cripple ... you're just like me ... you're just like me ... [*He breaks away, crying*] Oh, my God, I'm sorry, I'm sorry. Tom, please forgive me ... I didn't mean that ... I'm sorry, Tom, please, please ...

[*He very very gently touches and kisses her then draws her up to him and they hold each other tight.*]

I love you, I love you, I love you, I love you so much.

THOMASINA: Oh, Richard, I'm sorry, I'm sorry. I love you. I don't want to leave you. But I'm so scared ... I love you.

[*They continue to whisper love to each other as the lights very slowly fade to blackout.*]

THE END

[*As the audience exit, music is played: 'Oh my Love', Imagine L.P. — John Lennon.*]

FIND OUT MORE ABOUT
PENGUIN BOOKS

We publish the largest range of titles of any English language paperback publisher. As well as novels, crime and science fiction, humour, biography and large-format illustrated books, Penguin series include *Pelican Books* (on the arts, sciences and current affairs), *Penguin Reference Books*, *Penguin Classics*, *Penguin Modern Classics*, *Penguin English Library*, *Penguin Handbooks* (on subjects from cookery and gardening to sport), and *Puffin Books* for children. Other series cover a wide variety of interests from poetry to crosswords, and there are also several newly formed series – *Lives and Letters*, *King Penguin*, *Penguin American Library* and *Penguin Travel Library*.

We are an international publishing house, but for copyright reasons not every Penguin title is available in every country. To find out more about Penguins available in your country please write to our U.K. office – Dept EP, Penguin Books Ltd, Harmondsworth, Middlesex UB7 0DA – unless you live in one of the following areas:

In the U.S.A.: Dept DG, Penguin Books, 299 Murray Hill Parkway, East Rutherford, New Jersey 07073.

In Canada: Penguin Books Canada Ltd, 2801 John Street, Markham, Ontario L3R 1B4.

In Australia: Marketing Department, Penguin Books Australia Ltd, P.O. Box 257, Ringwood, Victoria 3134.

In New Zealand: Marketing Department, Penguin Books (N.Z.) Ltd, P.O. Box 4019, Auckland 10.

In India: Penguin Overseas Ltd, 706 Eros Apartments, 56 Nehru Place, New Delhi 110019.

PETER SHAFFER IN PENGUIN PLAYS

Amadeus

Winner of the *Evening Standard* Drama Award as best play of 1979, and of the *Plays and Players'* London Theatre Critics Award

'*Amadeus* may be a play inspired by music and death, but it fills the theatre with that mocking, heavenly silence that is the overwhelming terror of life' – *The New York Times*

'A marvellously engrossing and often amusing comic thriller, a feast for the eye and the ear . . .' – Steve Grant in the *Observer*

The Royal Hunt of the Sun

'One writer who manages to get right to the edge of experience . . . He manages to evoke the gods' – Colin Blakely

'This tremendous, this admirable, this profound, this enduring play' – Bernard Levin

THREE PLAYS

Equus
'Sensationally good' – Michael Billington in the *Guardian*

Shrivings
'A brilliant and deeply significant modern play' – *The Times*

Five Finger Exercise
'Peter Shaffer is one of our major playwrights, of a kind we need badly' – Eric Keown

FOUR PLAYS

The Private Ear/The Public Eye
'Pure comedy that is fresh and delightful . . . suddenly and immensely touching' – *Punch*

White Liars
Proves him 'a master of his art' – Harold Hobson

Black Comedy
'An uproarious farce . . . being written by Mr Shaffer it also has, over and above the demands of farce, wit and sophistication' – Bernard Levin

HUGH LEONARD IN PENGUIN PLAYS

DA/A LIFE/TIME WAS

Da

'A beguiling play about a son's need to come to terms with his father and himself . . . in a class with the best of Sean O'Casey' – *The New York Times*

A Life

'Even better than its famous predecessor (*Da*): as human and funny, but richer in texture and even more cannily aware of the sad complexity of life' – *Daily Telegraph*

Time Was

'Proves once again that he's Ireland's funniest playwright . . . snappy, witty, polished . . . Leonard's observations on Dublin suburbia are acidly accurate' – *Sunday Press* (Dublin)

Also by Hugh Leonard in Penguins

Home Before Night

A delightful evocation of his Dublin childhood in the thirties and forties, Hugh Leonard's autobiography is like an Irish *Cider With Rosie* – crammed with people and conversations, rich in poetry, full of love, laughter and rare pleasures.

'Entrancing . . . the playwright author's gift of language and apparently total recall make his account of growing up in the thirties and forties absolutely irresistible' – *Sunday Telegraph*

'Impossible to put down . . . a brilliant, multi-faceted gem' – *Hibernia*

'An unqualified delight . . . (he has) a marvellous eye for character, the ability to weave show-stopping funny stories into larger narrative, and to recreate the past with the sensuous immediacy of childhood' – Irving Wardle in *Books and Bookmen*

'Superb . . . moving and very funny' – William Trevor